CONTENTS

A Precious Quest

Jason's story began when his father, Aeson, was dethroned as king of Iolcus by an evil half brother called Pelias. To avoid their fate, Jason's parents spirited him away from their dungeon to be raised by a centaur, Chiron, on Mount Pelion.

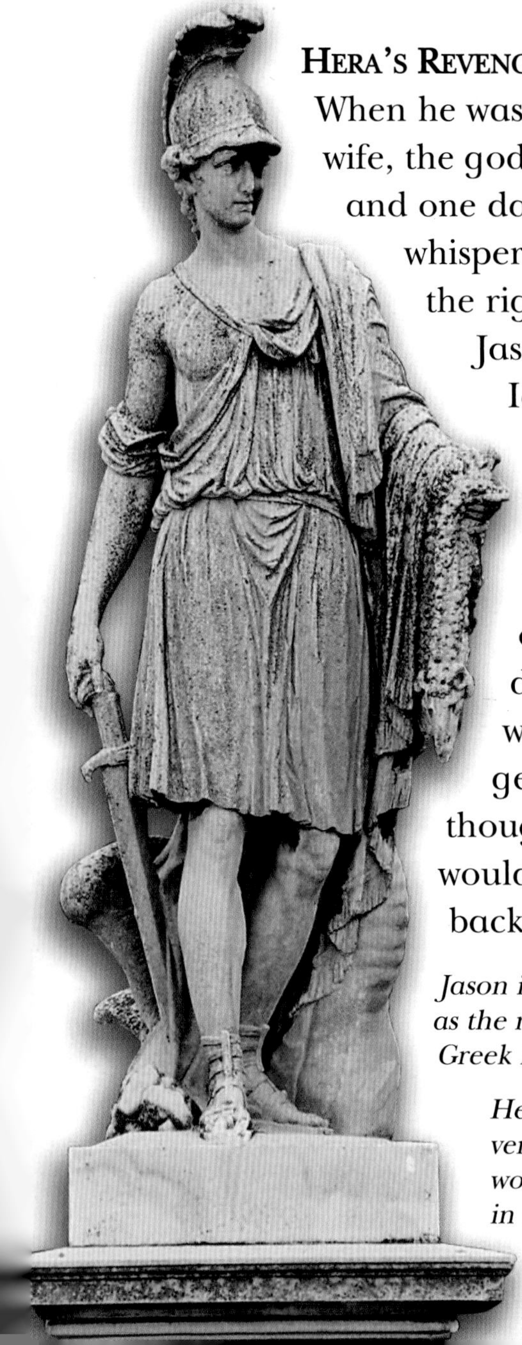

Hera's Revenge

When he was young, Pelias had angered Zeus's wife, the goddess Hera. She had sworn revenge, and one day when Jason was grown, she whispered in his ear as he slept, "You are the rightful heir to the throne."

Jason made his way to the palace of Iolcus and demanded his uncle give up the throne. Pelias agreed on the condition that Jason find and bring back the fabled golden fleece. Wishing to prove himself, Jason at once agreed. Pelias was secretly delighted—the fleece was so difficult to get to that he thought Jason wouldn't make it back alive.

Jason is often portrayed as the most human of Greek heroes.

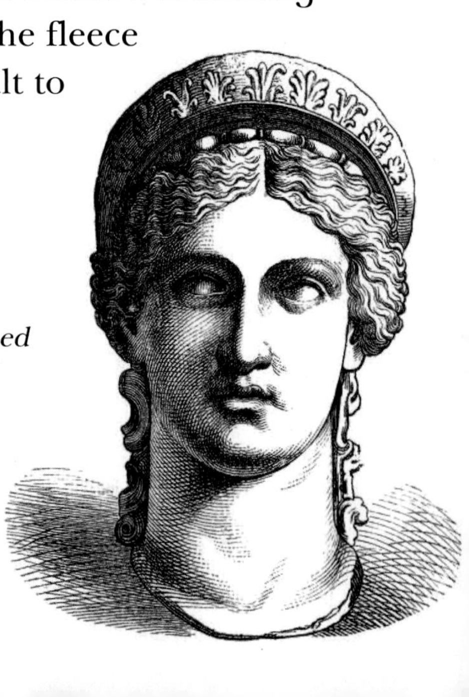

Hera's need for vengeance would aid Jason in his quest.

GRAPHIC MYTHICAL HEROES

JASON
AND THE ARGONAUTS

BY GARY JEFFREY
ILLUSTRATED BY DHEERAJ VERMA

Gareth Stevens
Publishing

Please visit our website, www.garethstevens.com.
For a free color catalog of all our high-quality books,
call toll free 1-800-542-2595 or fax 1-877-542-2596.

Library of Congress Cataloging-in-Publication Data

Jeffrey, Gary.
Jason and the Argonauts / Gary Jeffrey.
p. cm. — (Graphic mythical heroes)
Includes index.
ISBN 978-1-4339-7516-5 (pbk.)
ISBN 978-1-4339-7517-2 (6-pack)
ISBN 978-1-4339-7515-8 (library binding)
1. Jason (Greek mythology)—Juvenile literature. 2. Argonauts (Greek
mythology)—Juvenile literature. I. Title.
BL820.A8J44 2012
398.20938'02—dc23
                                                        2011045595

First Edition

Published in 2013 by
Gareth Stevens Publishing
111 East 14th Street, Suite 349
New York, NY 10003

Copyright © 2013 David West Books

Designed by David West Books

Printed in China

CPSIA compliance information: Batch #DWS12GS: For further information contact Gareth Stevens, New York, New York at 1-800-542-2595.

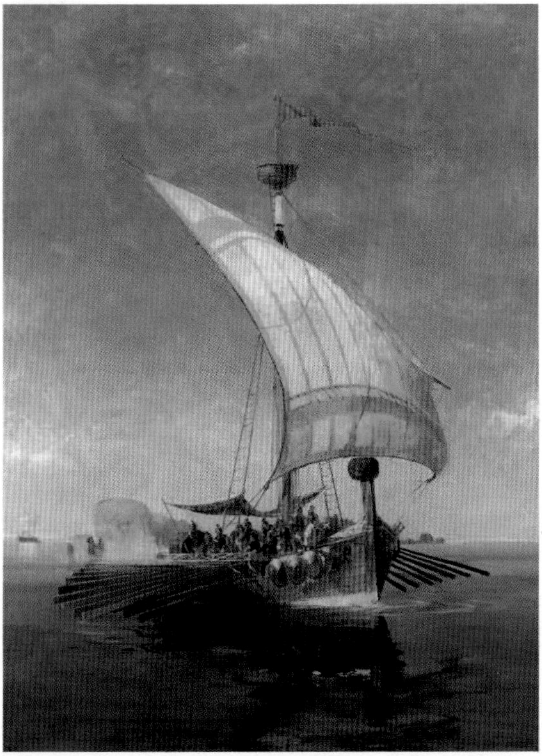

PREPARING FOR ADVENTURE

News of Jason's quest attracted many demigods and princes to Iolcus. They discussed how to get to the distant land of Colchis, where the fleece was rumored to be kept.

A fine ship, called the Argo, was built and crewed by 50 of the heroes now known as the Argonauts.

A 19th-century painting which shows the Argo on its eastward journey across the Aegean Sea.

THE JOURNEY TO COLCHIS

They passed by many islands. Landing on one near Mysia, they were attacked by six-armed ogres called Gegenees. Luckily the Argonauts won the day. When they arrived in Thrace, they saved a seer called Phineas from being tormented by flying monsters called Harpies.

In return, Phineas told them how to use a dove to get through the deadly clashing rocks—the gateway to the unexplored sea that led to Colchis...

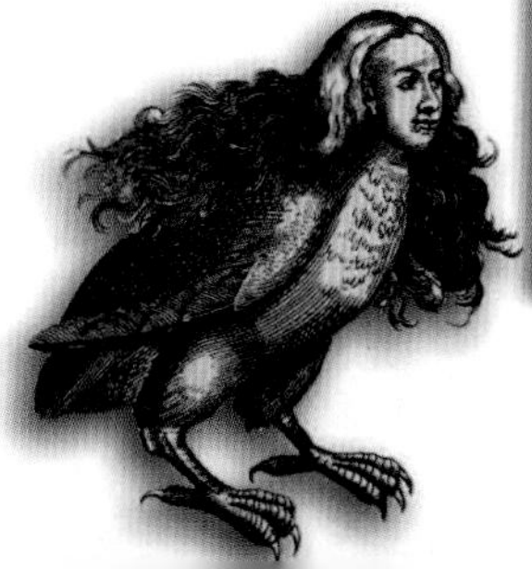

Harpies had the body of a bird with the head of a woman.

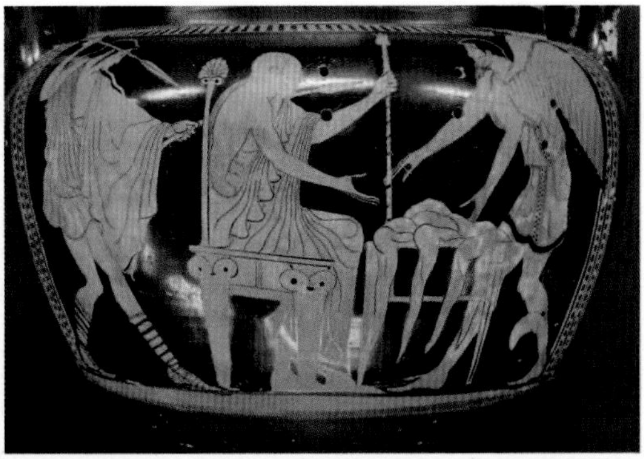

Winged Argonauts called Boreads drove the Harpies away from Phineas's table.

Jason and the Golden Fleece

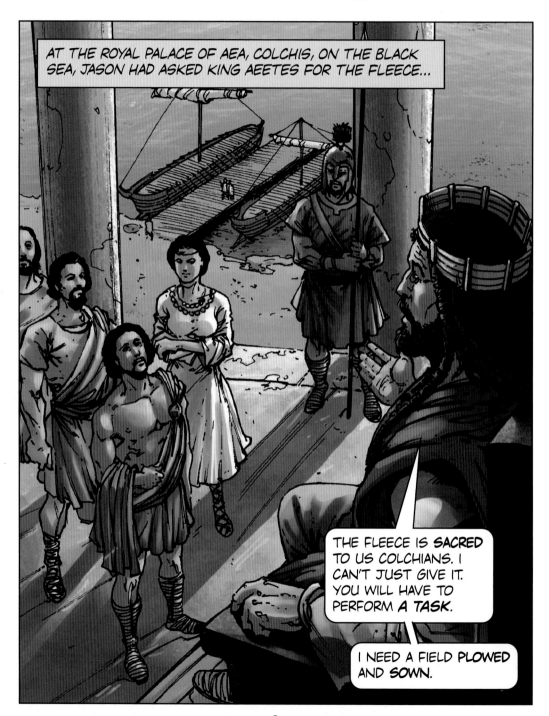

AT THE ROYAL PALACE OF AEA, COLCHIS, ON THE BLACK SEA, JASON HAD ASKED KING AEETES FOR THE FLEECE...

THE FLEECE IS **SACRED** TO US COLCHIANS. I CAN'T JUST GIVE IT. YOU WILL HAVE TO PERFORM **A TASK**.

I NEED A FIELD **PLOWED** AND **SOWN**.

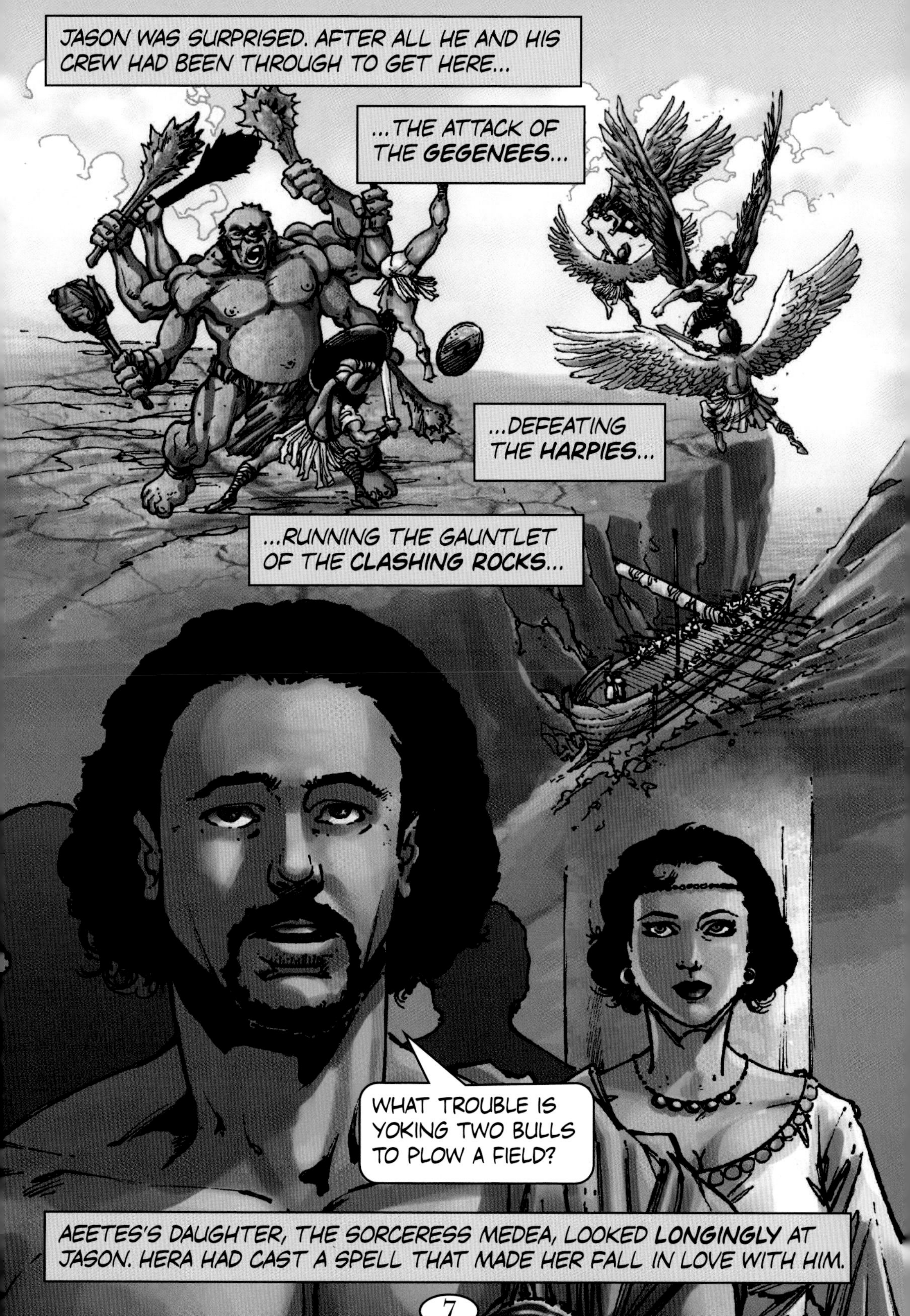
JASON WAS SURPRISED. AFTER ALL HE AND HIS CREW HAD BEEN THROUGH TO GET HERE...
...THE ATTACK OF THE GEGENEES...
...DEFEATING THE HARPIES...
...RUNNING THE GAUNTLET OF THE CLASHING ROCKS...
WHAT TROUBLE IS YOKING TWO BULLS TO PLOW A FIELD?
AEETES'S DAUGHTER, THE SORCERESS MEDEA, LOOKED LONGINGLY AT JASON. HERA HAD CAST A SPELL THAT MADE HER FALL IN LOVE WITH HIM.

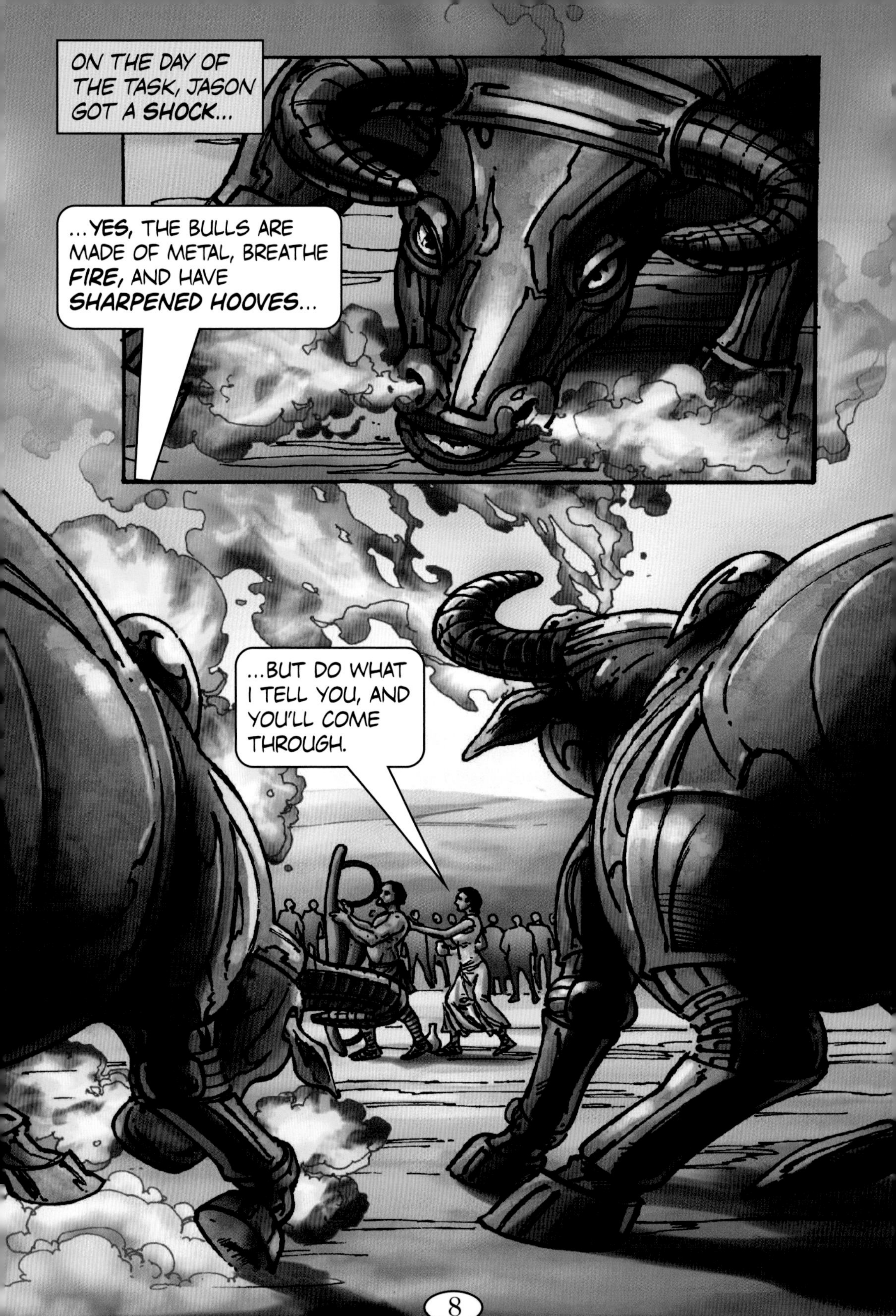
ON THE DAY OF THE TASK, JASON GOT A SHOCK...
...YES, THE BULLS ARE MADE OF METAL, BREATHE FIRE, AND HAVE SHARPENED HOOVES...
...BUT DO WHAT I TELL YOU, AND YOU'LL COME THROUGH.

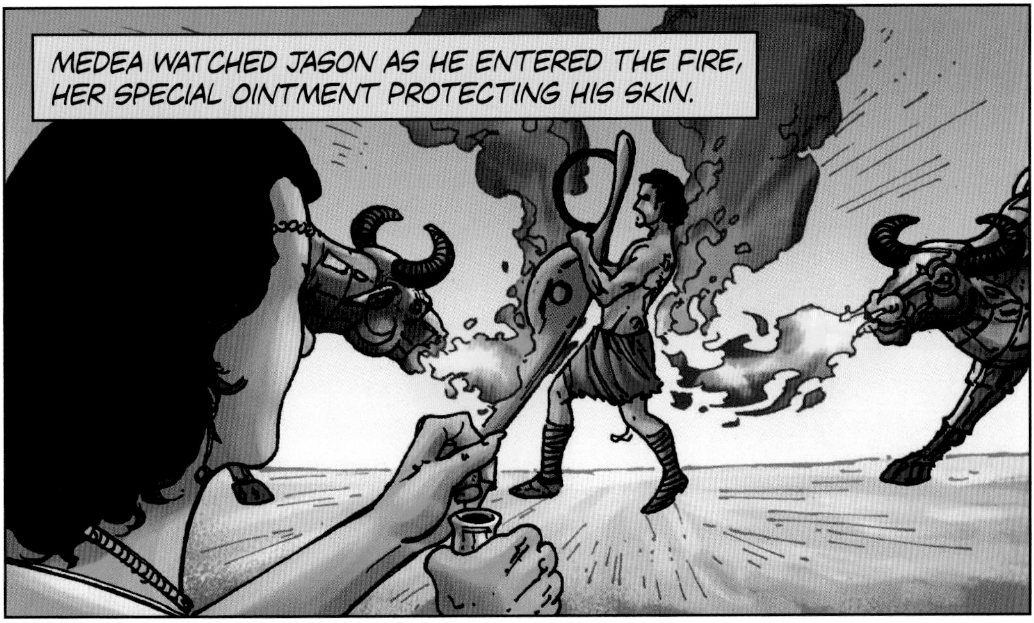
MEDEA WATCHED JASON AS HE ENTERED THE FIRE, HER SPECIAL OINTMENT PROTECTING HIS SKIN.

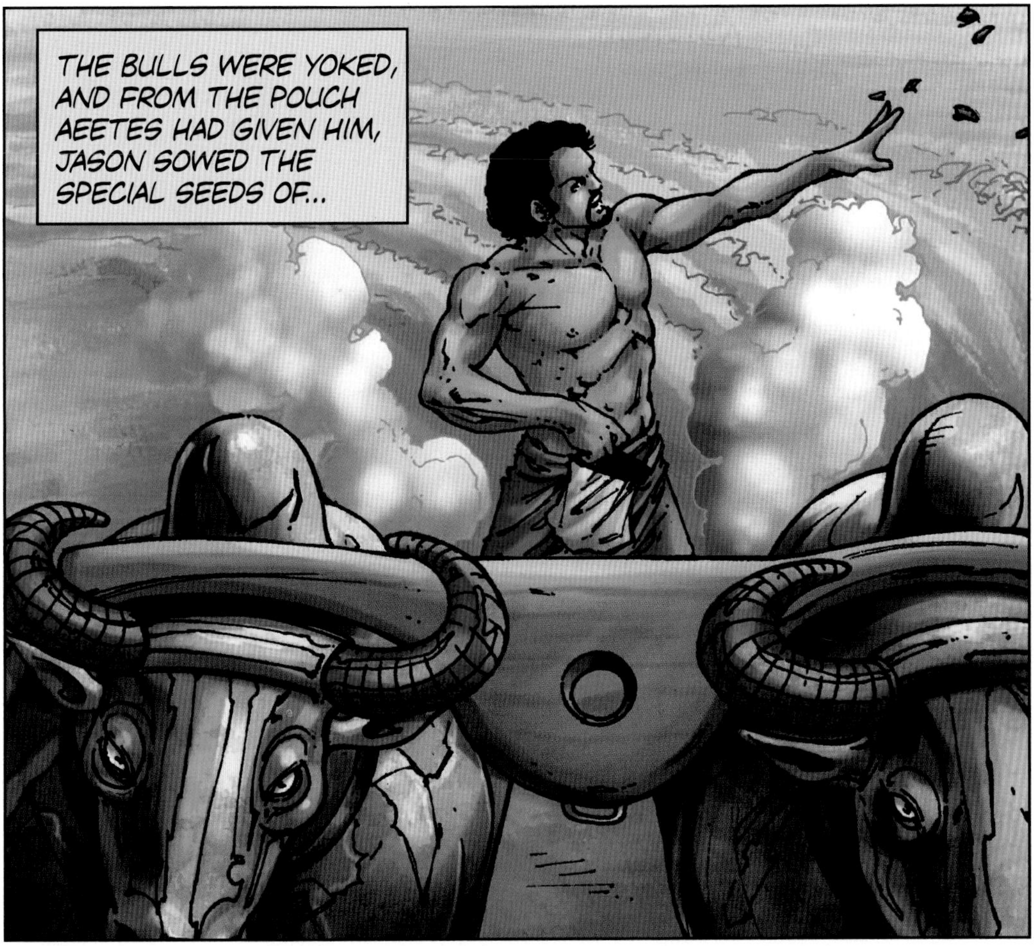
THE BULLS WERE YOKED, AND FROM THE POUCH AEETES HAD GIVEN HIM, JASON SOWED THE SPECIAL SEEDS OF...

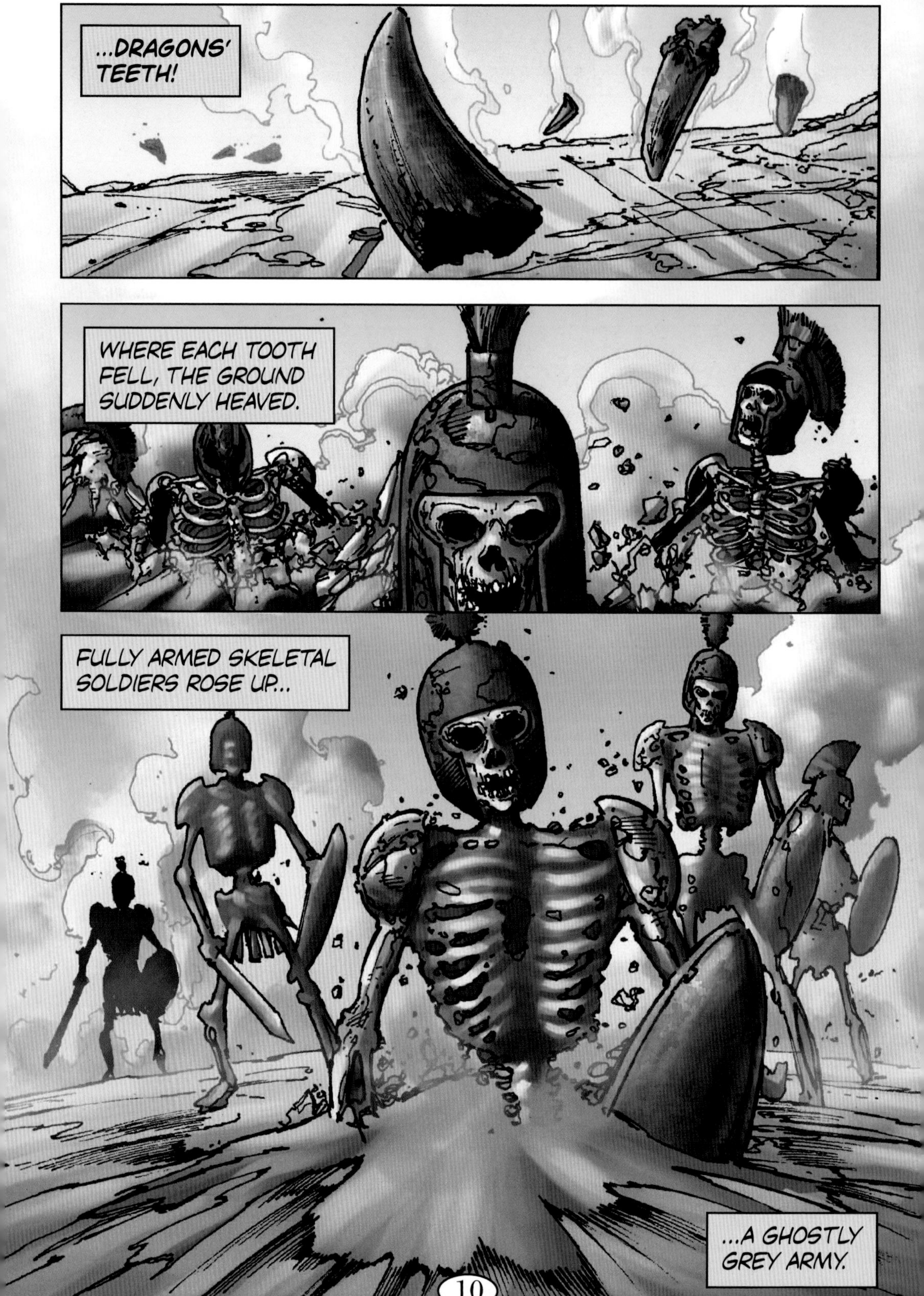
...DRAGONS' TEETH!
WHERE EACH TOOTH FELL, THE GROUND SUDDENLY HEAVED.
FULLY ARMED SKELETAL SOLDIERS ROSE UP...
...A GHOSTLY GREY ARMY.

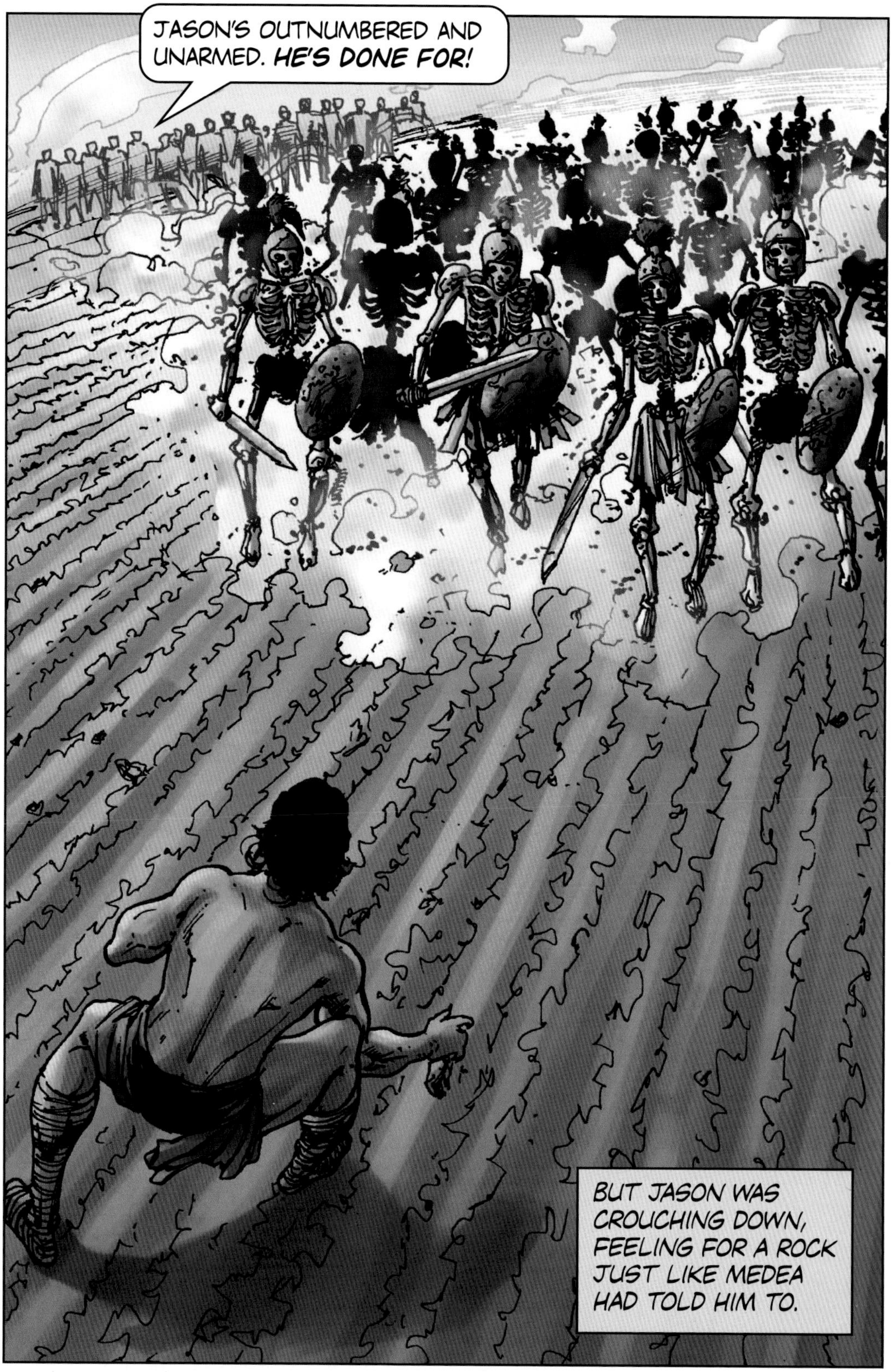

JASON'S OUTNUMBERED AND UNARMED. **HE'S DONE FOR!**
BUT JASON WAS CROUCHING DOWN, FEELING FOR A ROCK JUST LIKE MEDEA HAD TOLD HIM TO.

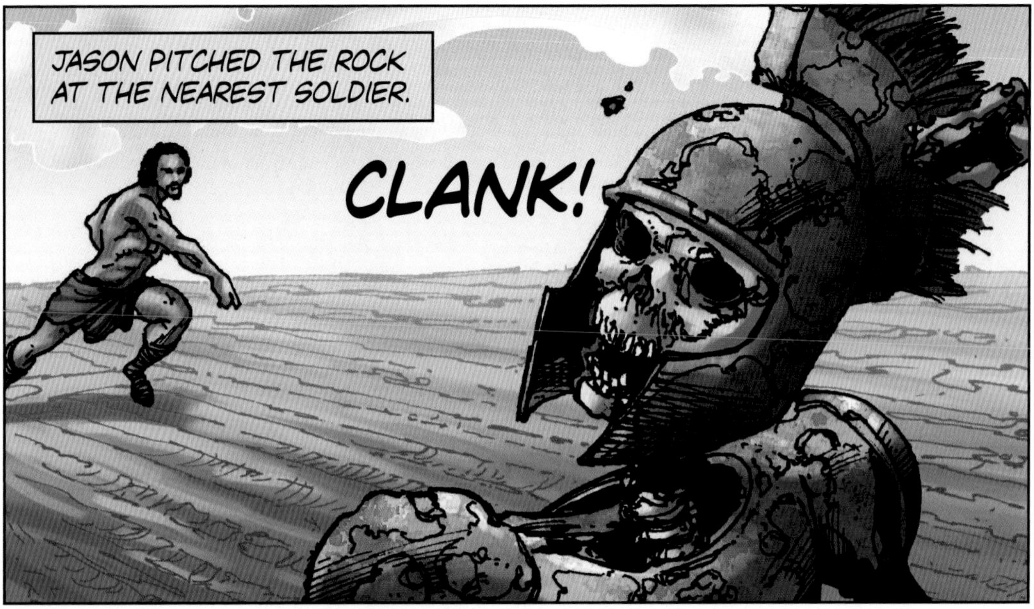
JASON PITCHED THE ROCK AT THE NEAREST SOLDIER.
CLANK!

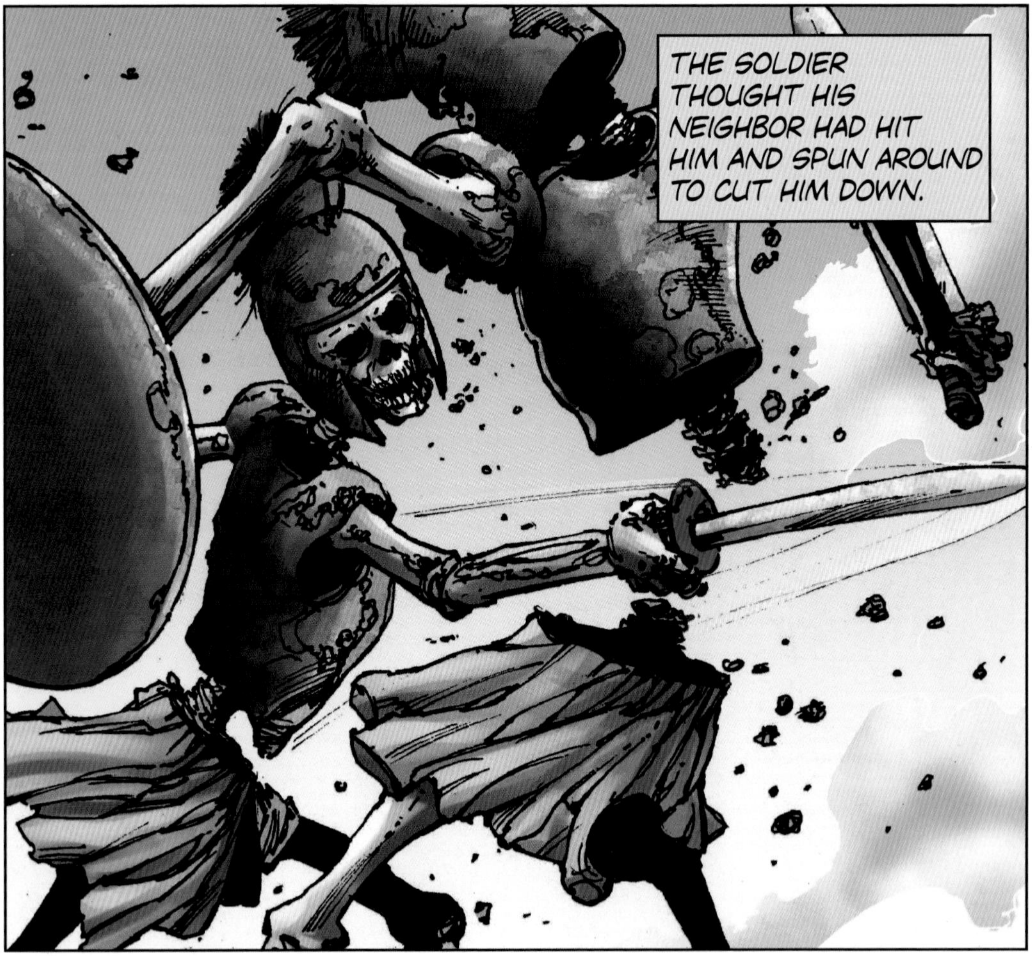
THE SOLDIER THOUGHT HIS NEIGHBOR HAD HIT HIM AND SPUN AROUND TO CUT HIM DOWN.

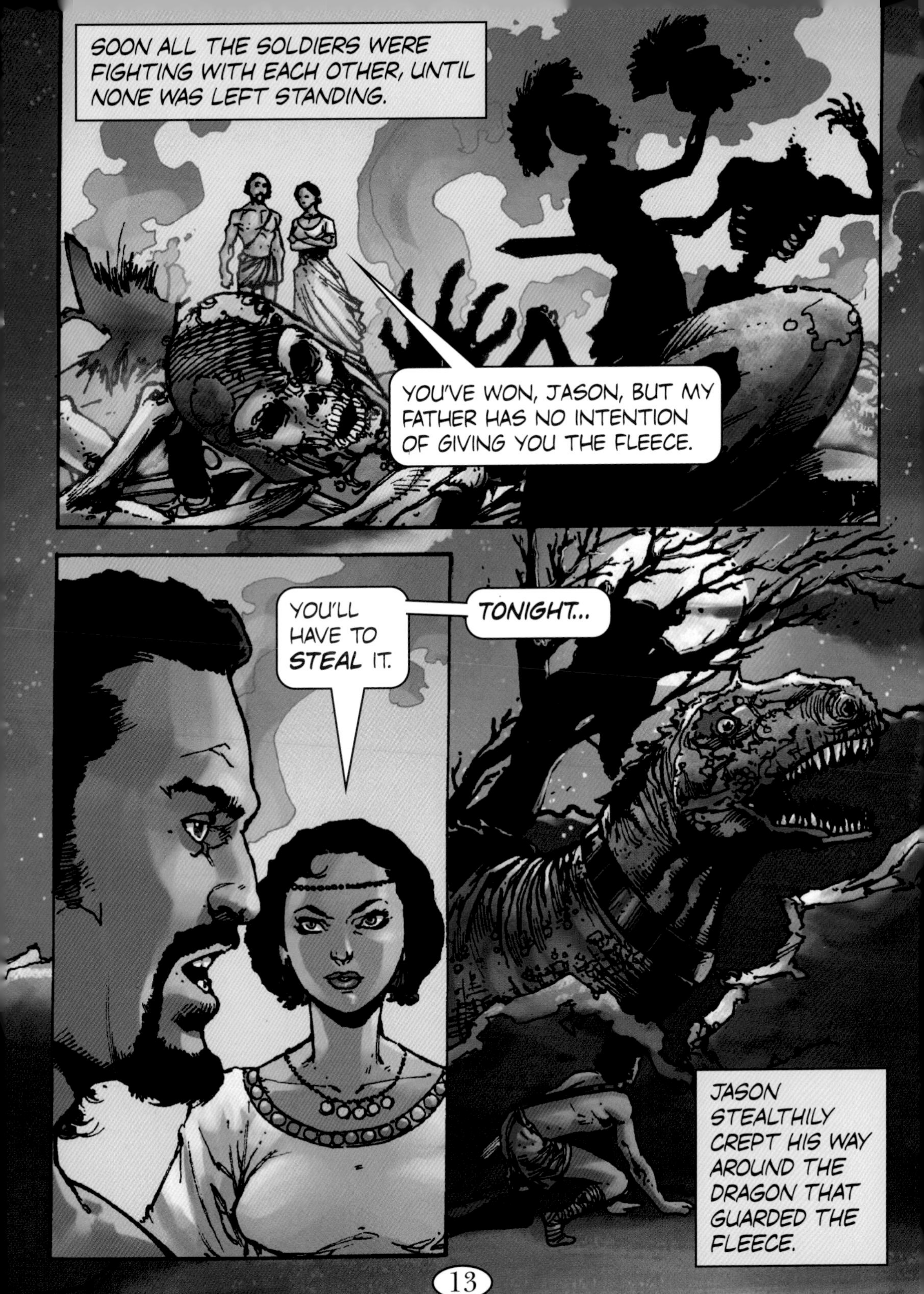
SOON ALL THE SOLDIERS WERE FIGHTING WITH EACH OTHER, UNTIL NONE WAS LEFT STANDING.
YOU'VE WON, JASON, BUT MY FATHER HAS NO INTENTION OF GIVING YOU THE FLEECE.
YOU'LL HAVE TO STEAL IT.
TONIGHT...
JASON STEALTHILY CREPT HIS WAY AROUND THE DRAGON THAT GUARDED THE FLEECE.

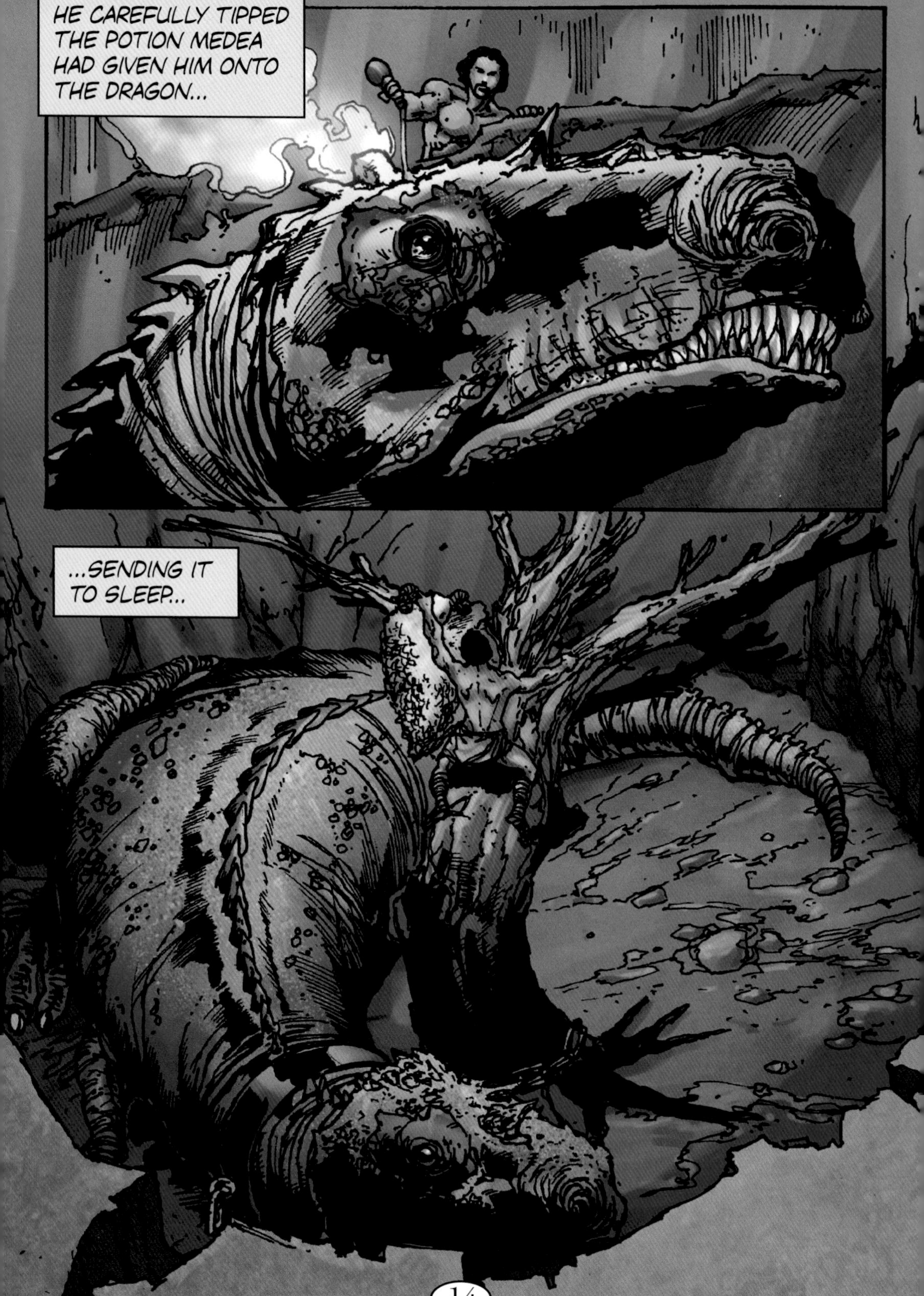
HE CAREFULLY TIPPED THE POTION MEDEA HAD GIVEN HIM ONTO THE DRAGON...
...SENDING IT TO SLEEP...

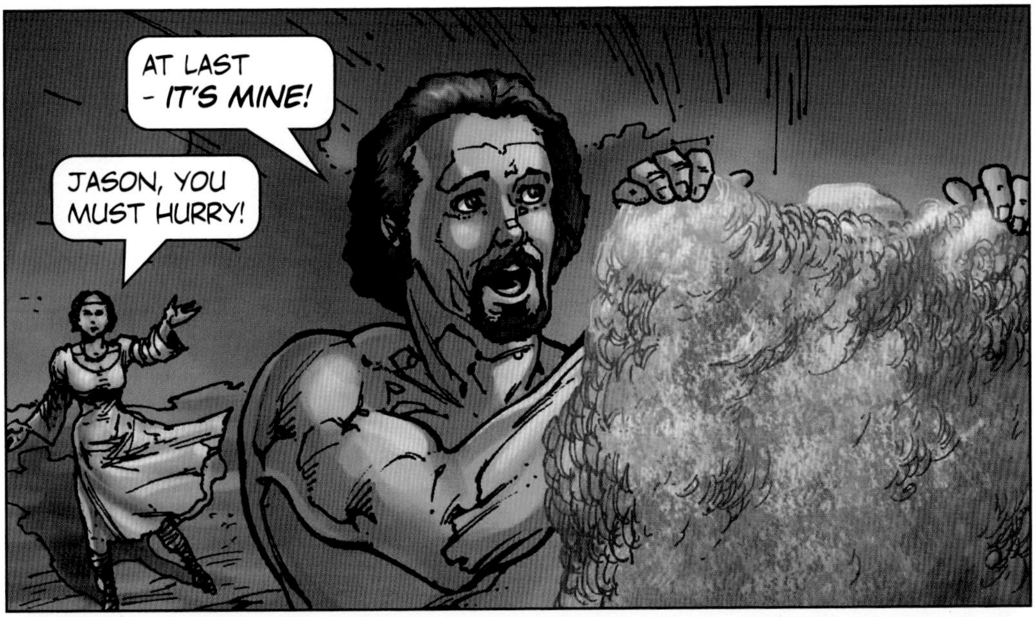
AT LAST - IT'S MINE!
JASON, YOU MUST HURRY!

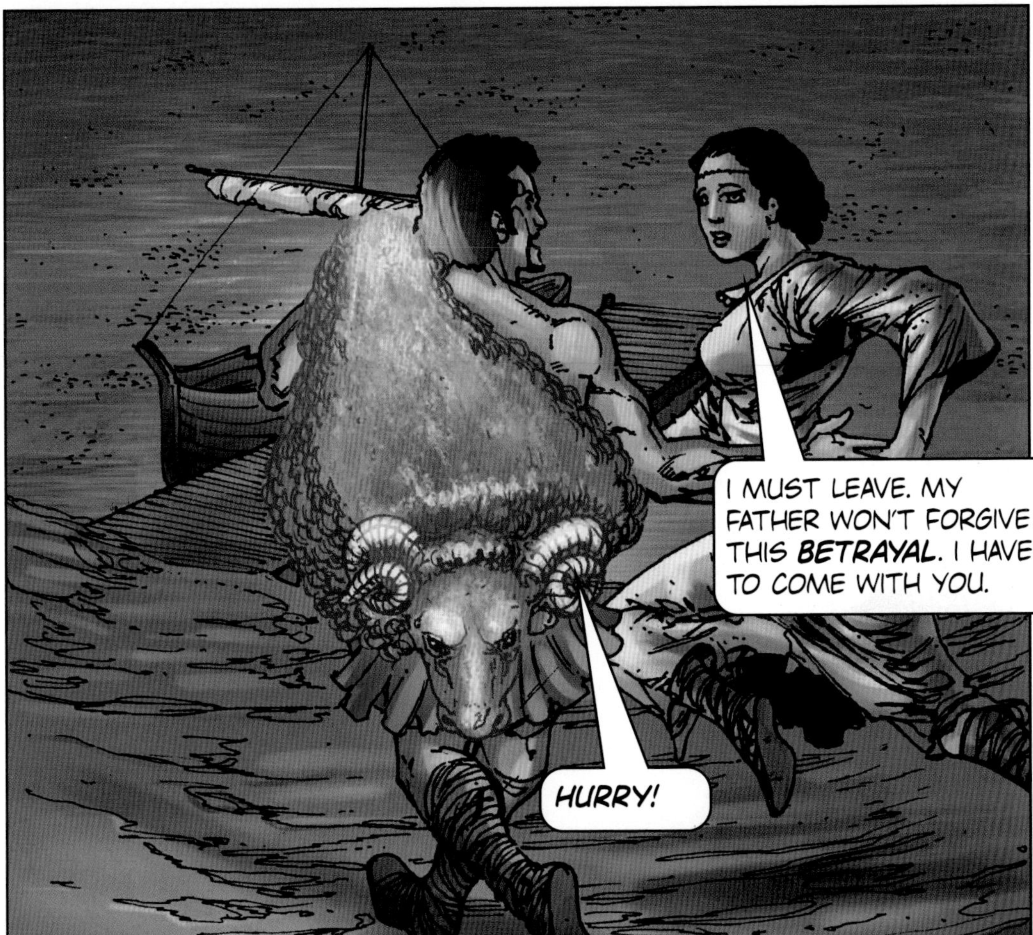
I MUST LEAVE. MY FATHER WON'T FORGIVE THIS BETRAYAL. I HAVE TO COME WITH YOU.
HURRY!

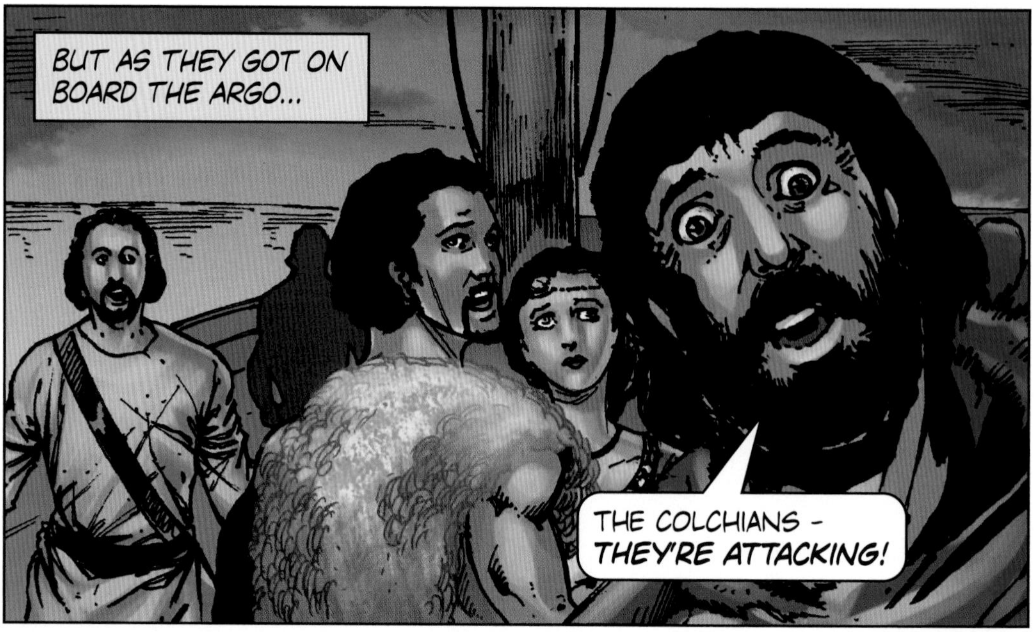
BUT AS THEY GOT ON BOARD THE ARGO...
THE COLCHIANS - THEY'RE ATTACKING!

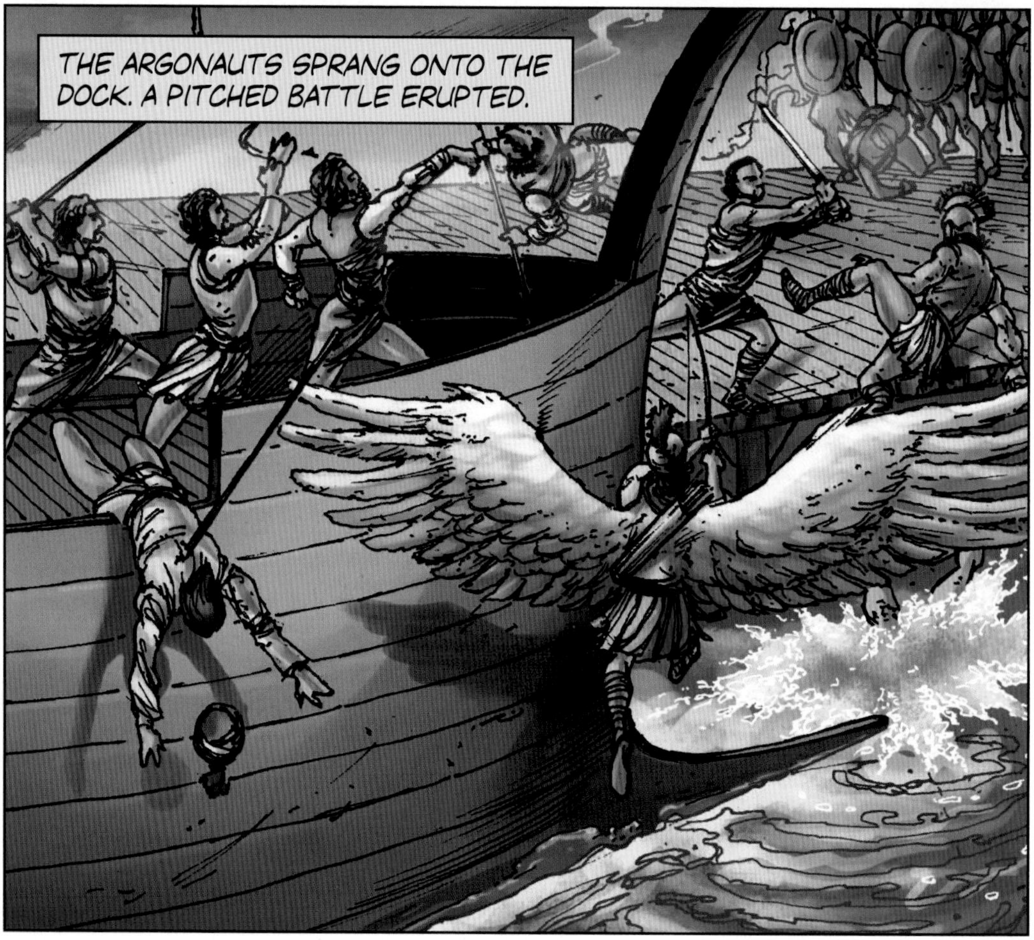
THE ARGONAUTS SPRANG ONTO THE DOCK. A PITCHED BATTLE ERUPTED.

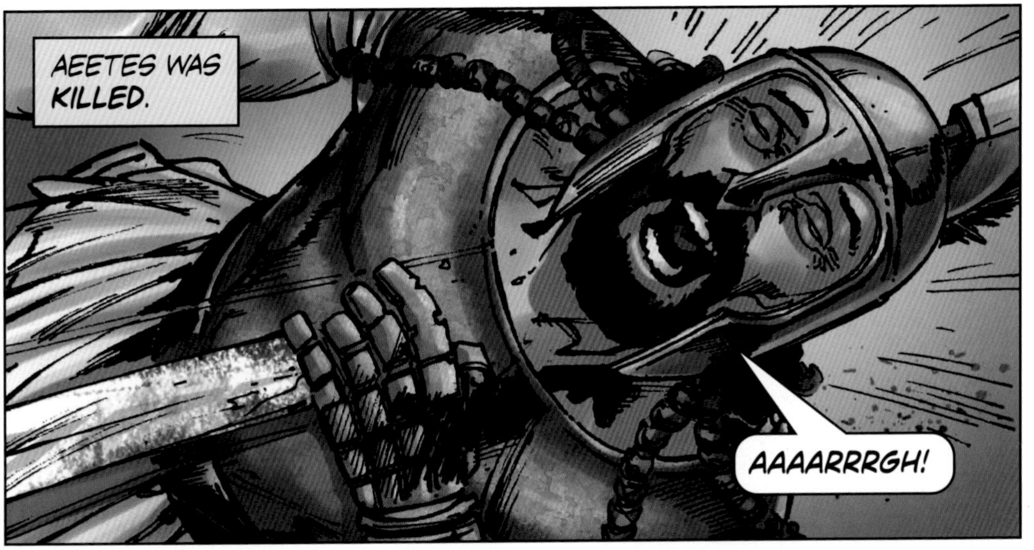
AEETES WAS KILLED.
AAAARRRGH!

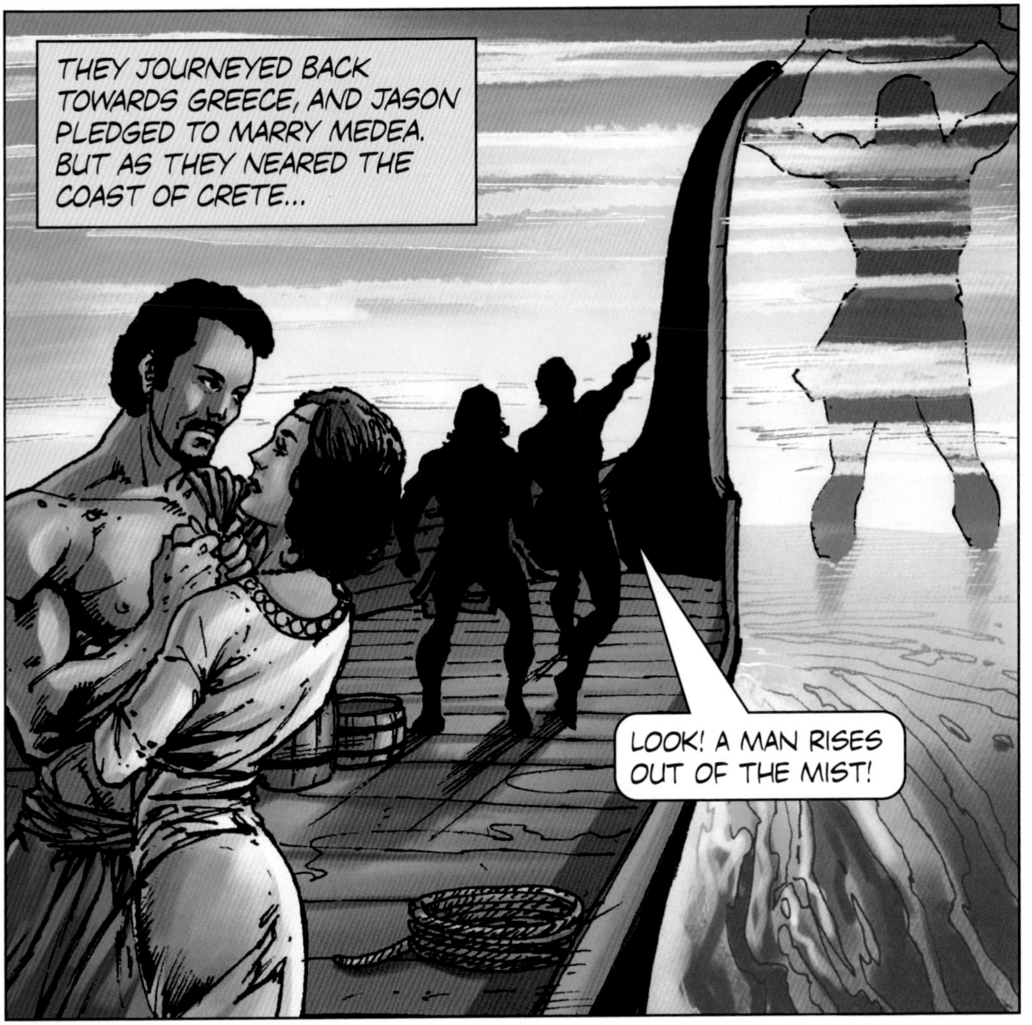
THEY JOURNEYED BACK TOWARDS GREECE, AND JASON PLEDGED TO MARRY MEDEA. BUT AS THEY NEARED THE COAST OF CRETE...
LOOK! A MAN RISES OUT OF THE MIST!

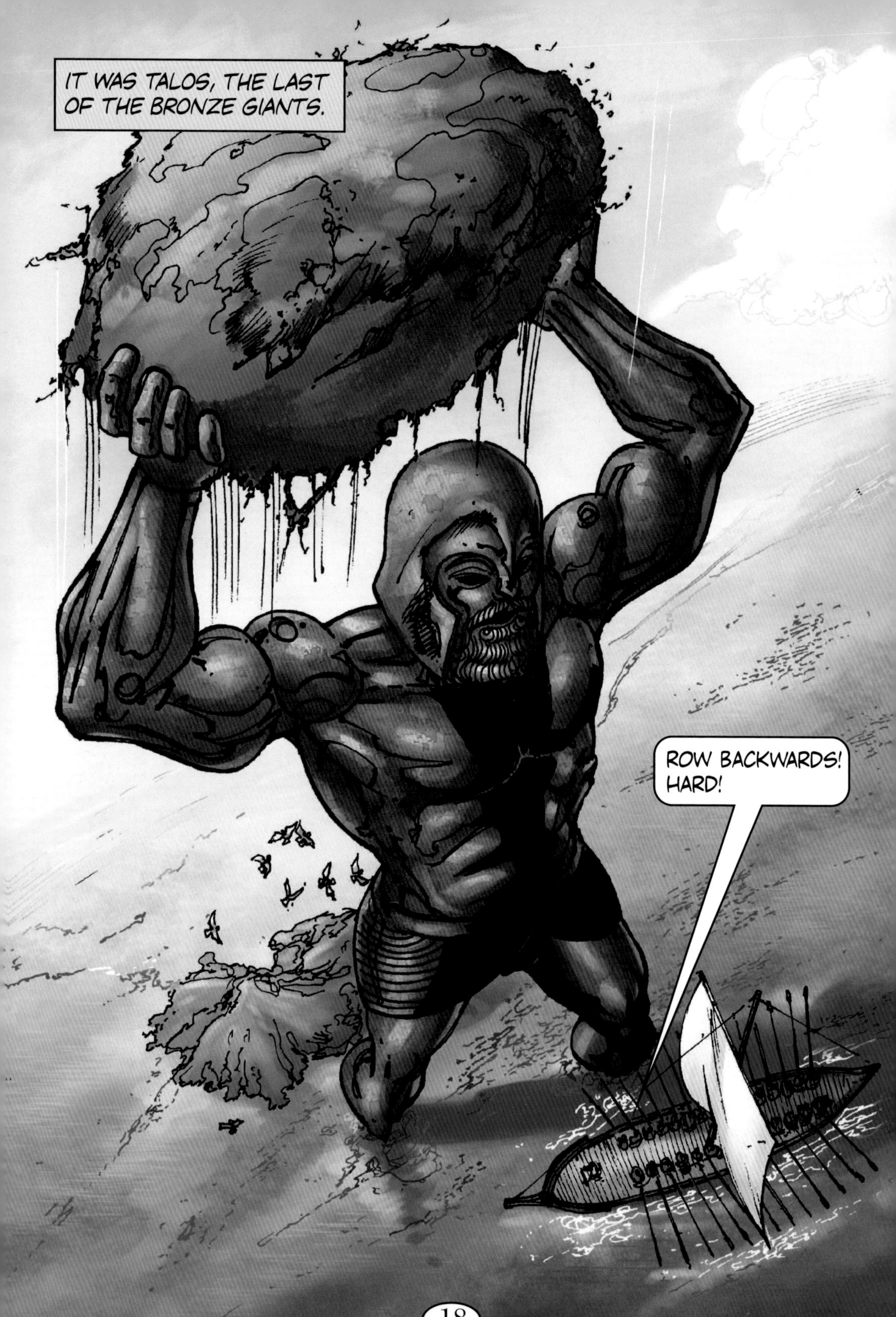
IT WAS TALOS, THE LAST OF THE BRONZE GIANTS.
ROW BACKWARDS! HARD!

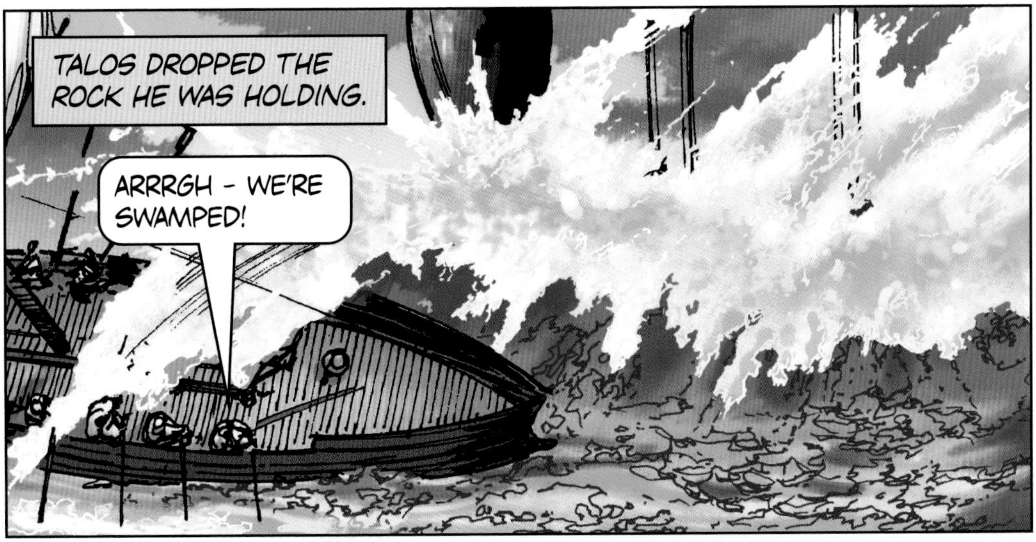
TALOS DROPPED THE ROCK HE WAS HOLDING.
ARRRGH - WE'RE SWAMPED!

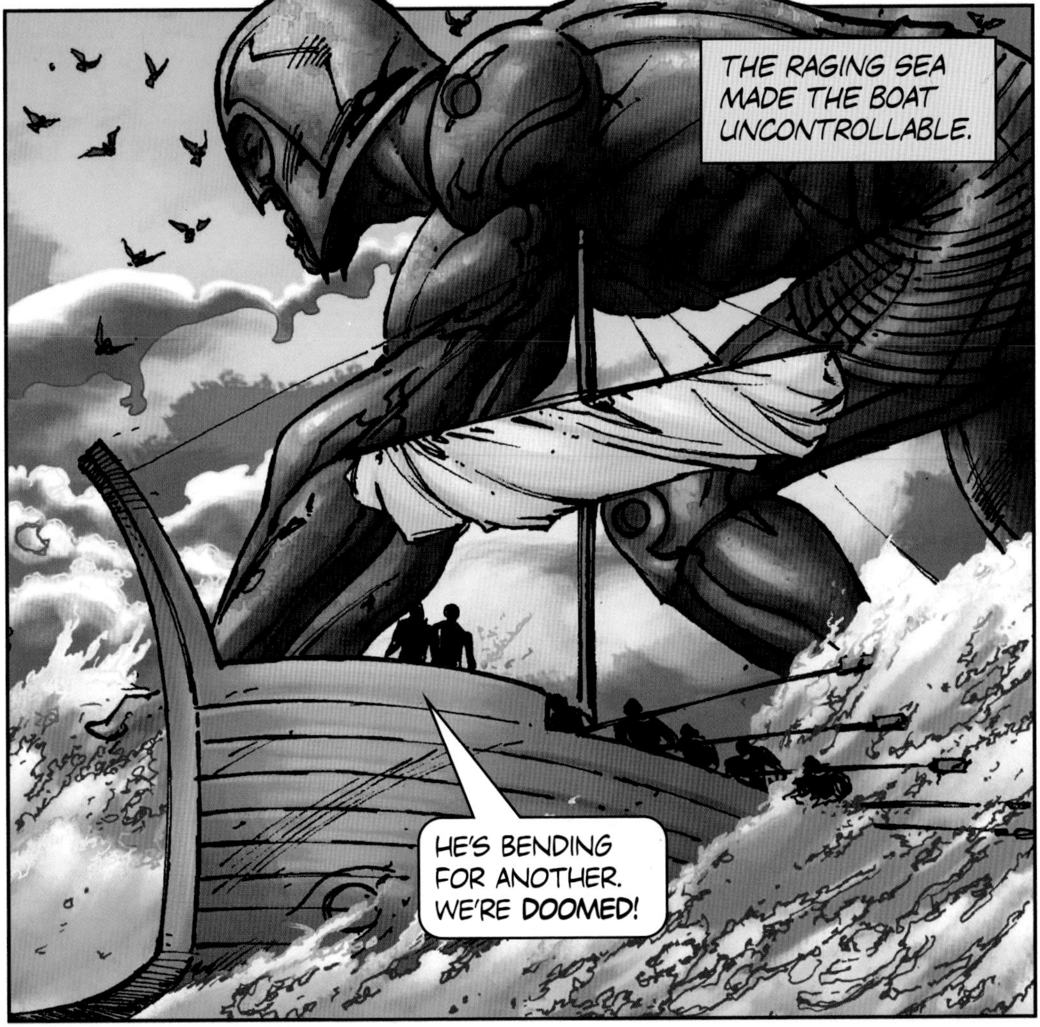
THE RAGING SEA MADE THE BOAT UNCONTROLLABLE.
HE'S BENDING FOR ANOTHER. WE'RE DOOMED!

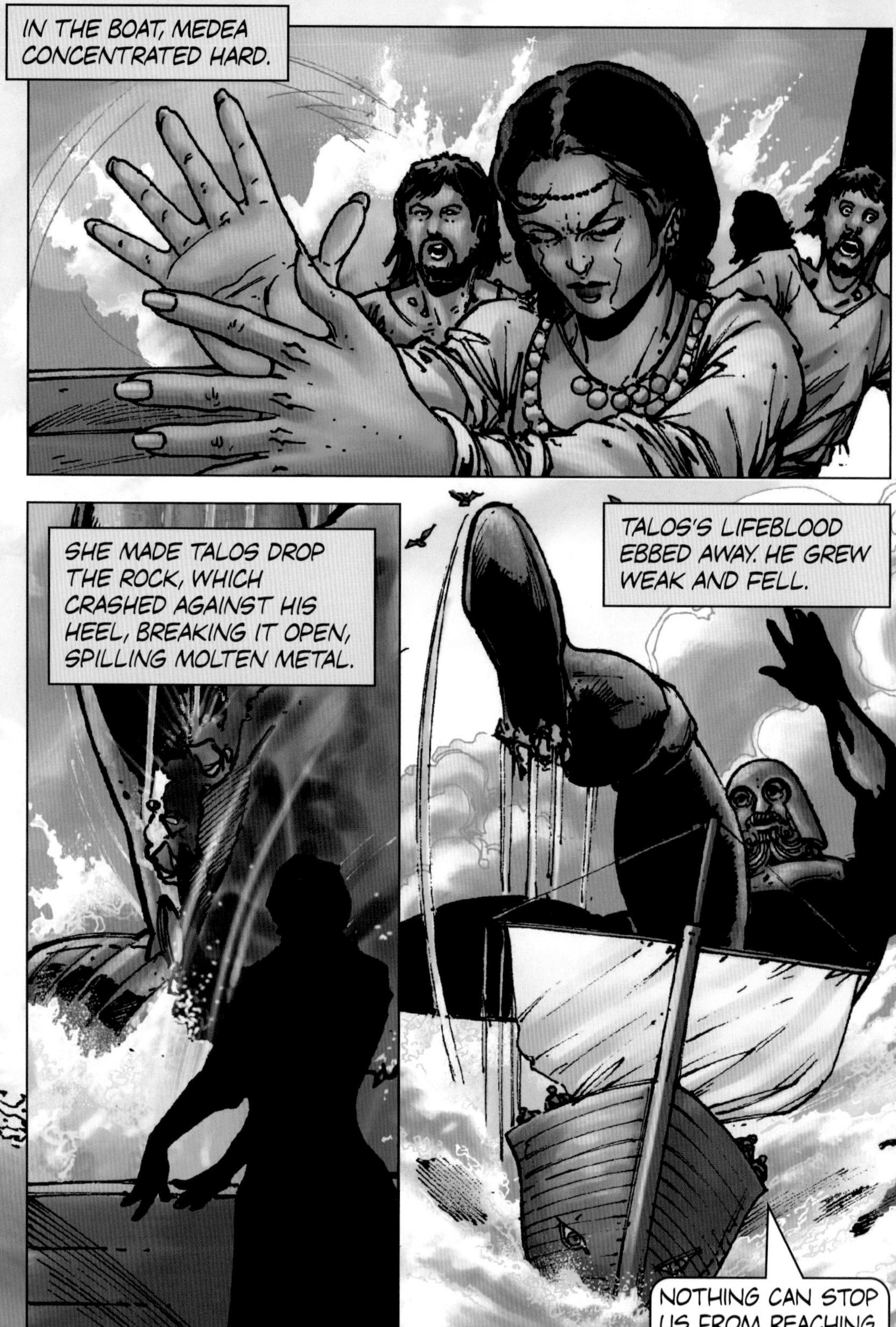

IN THE BOAT, MEDEA CONCENTRATED HARD.
SHE MADE TALOS DROP THE ROCK, WHICH CRASHED AGAINST HIS HEEL, BREAKING IT OPEN, SPILLING MOLTEN METAL.
TALOS'S LIFEBLOOD EBBED AWAY. HE GREW WEAK AND FELL.
NOTHING CAN STOP US FROM REACHING IOLCUS NOW!

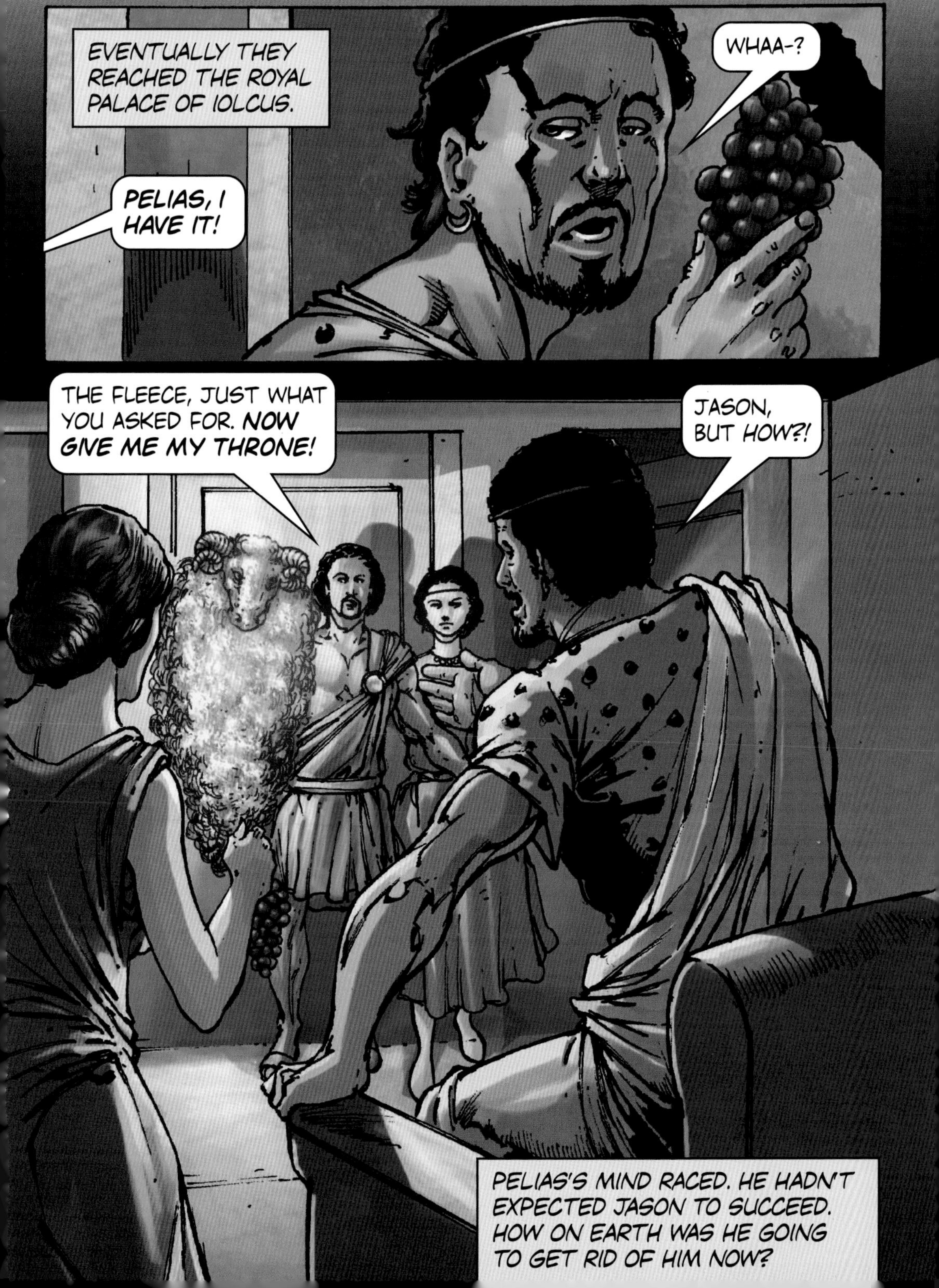
EVENTUALLY THEY REACHED THE ROYAL PALACE OF IOLCUS.
WHAA-?
PELIAS, I HAVE IT!
THE FLEECE, JUST WHAT YOU ASKED FOR. NOW GIVE ME MY THRONE!
JASON, BUT HOW?!
PELIAS'S MIND RACED. HE HADN'T EXPECTED JASON TO SUCCEED. HOW ON EARTH WAS HE GOING TO GET RID OF HIM NOW?

Revenge Served Cold

Watching Pelias, Medea sensed the danger Jason was in and vowed to protect him. It was all part of Hera's plan. She had guided the sorceress to Iolcus expressly to kill Pelias.

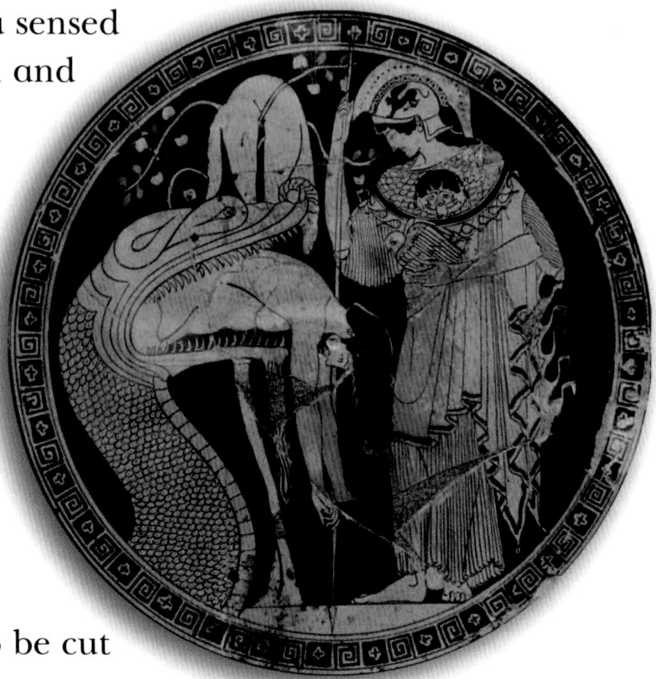

The story of Jason as imagined on a cup from the 5th century BC, 700 years after the Greeks believed the events happened.

Pot Luck

Pelias's great age gave Medea an idea. She gathered Pelias's daughters together and called for an old ram to be cut into pieces and put into a pot. She poured in a magic potion, and out sprang a new lamb! "With this potion, I can make your father young again," she told the daughters, but they must prepare the king in the same way.

Pelias's daughters wanted their father to be young again, so they stole into his room, killed him, cut him into pieces, and put him in the pot. Medea added the potion, but it was fake—the daughters had slain their father for nothing. Hera had won.

Jason and Medea fled from Iolcus to Corinth, where they married and settled down.

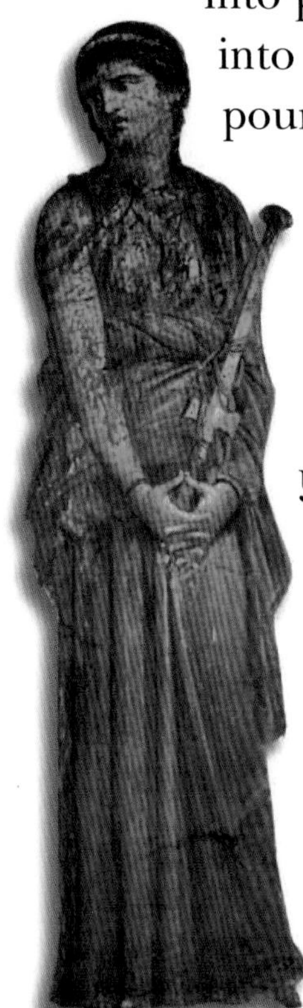

The marriage did not last. Jason left Medea for Glauce, the king of Corinth's daughter. Medea (left) became a leading character in classical tragedies.

Glossary

betrayal The act of breaking a promise or going against one's word.

centaur A mythical creature with the body of a horse and the torso of a man.

ebbed Gradually retreated or faded away.

heir The person next in line to be king.

molten The state of a solid, often metal, that is heated to the point of becoming liquid.

ointment A lotion-like medicine that protects or heals the skin.

pledged Promised.

quest A long journey in search of something.

raging Moving violently up and down.

running the gauntlet Undertaking a challenging task.

seer A person who has the ability to see the future.

stealthily In a sneaky manner.

tragedies Very sad, unfortunate occurrences, or stories that tell about such occurrences.

Index